The Missions: California's Heritage

# MISSION SAN CARLOS BORROMEO de CARMELO

by

Mary Null Boulé

Book Two in a series of twenty-one

DEAR READER,

You will find an outline of this chapter's important topics at the back of the booklet. It is there for you to use in writing a report or giving an oral report on this mission.

If you first read the booklet completely, then you can use the outline as a guide to write your report in your own words, instead of copying sentences from the chapter.

> Good luck, read carefully,
> and use your own words.
> MNB

Cover illustration: Ellen Grim

# The Missions: California's Heritage

# MISSION SAN CARLOS BORROMEO

# de CARMELO

by

## Mary Null Boulé

Merryant Publishing
Vashon, Washington

Book Two in a series of twenty-one

With special thanks to Msgr. Francis J. Weber, Archivist of the Los Angeles Catholic Diocese for his encouragement and expertise in developing this series.

*This series is dedicated to my sister, Nancy Null Kenyon, whose editing skills and support were so freely given.*

Library of Congress Catalog Card Number: 89-90967

**ISBN: 1-877599-01-8**

Father Junípero Serra

## INTRODUCTION

*Building of a mission church involved everyone in the mission community. Priests were engineers and architects; Native Americans did the construction. Mission Indian in front is pouring adobe mix into a brick form. Bricks were then dried in the sun.*

## FATHER SERRA AND THE MISSIONS: AN INTRODUCTION

The year was 1769. On the east coast of what would soon become the United States, the thirteen original colonies were making ready to break away from England. On the west coast of our continent, however, there could be found only untamed land inhabited by Native Americans, or Indians. Although European explorers had sailed up and down the coast in their ships, no one but American Indians had explored the length of this land on foot . . . until now.

To this wild, beautiful country came a group of adventurous men from New Spain, as Mexico was then called. They were following the orders of their king, King Charles III of Spain.

One of the men was a Spanish missionary named Fray Junípero Serra. He had been given a tremendous job; especially since he was fifty-six years old, an old man in those days. King Charles III had ordered mission settlements to be built along the coast of Alta (Upper) California and it was Fr. Serra's task to carry out the king's wishes.

Father Serra had been born in the tiny village of Petra

the island of Mallorca, Spain. He had done such an excellent job of teaching and working with the Indians in Mexican missions, the governor of New Spain had suggested to the king that Fr. Serra do the same with the Indians of Alta California. Hard-working Fray Serra was helped by Don Gaspár de Portolá, newly chosen governor of Alta California, and two other Franciscan priests who had grown up with Fr. Serra in Mallorca, Father Fermin Lasuén and Father Francisco Palóu.

There were several reasons why men had been told to build settlements along the coast of this unexplored country. First, missions would help keep the land as Spanish territory. Spain wanted to be sure the rest of the world knew it owned this rich land. Second, missions were to be built near harbors so towns would grow there. Ships from other countries could then stop to trade with the Spaniards, but these travelers could not try to claim the land for themselves. Third, missions were a good way to turn Indians into Christian, hard-working people.

It would be nice if we could write here that everything went well; that twenty-one missions immediately sprang up along the coast. Unfortunately, all did not go well. It would take fifty-four years to build all the California Missions. During those fifty-four years many people died from Indian attacks, sickness, and starvation. Earthquakes and fires constantly ruined mission buildings, which then had to be built all over again. Fr. Serra calmly overcame each problem as it happened, as did those priests who followed him.

When a weary Fray Serra finally died in 1784, he had founded nine missions from San Diego to Monterey and had arranged the building of many more. Fr. Lasuén continued Fr. Serra's work, adding eight more missions to the California mission chain. The remaining four missions were founded in later years.

Originally, plans had been to place missions a hard day's walk from each other. Many of them were really quite far apart. Travelers truly struggled to go from one mission to another along the 650 miles of walking road known as El Camino Real, The Royal Highway. Today keen eyes will sometimes see tall, curved poles with bells hanging from them sitting by the side of streets and highways. These bell poles are marking a part of the old El Camino Real.

At first Spanish soldiers were put in charge of the towns which grew up near each mission. The priests were told to handle only the mission and its properties. It did not take long to realize the soldiers were not kind and gentle leaders. Many were uneducated and did not have the understanding they should have had in dealing with people. So the padres came to be in charge of not only the mission, but of the townspeople and even of the soldiers.

The first missions at San Diego and Monterey were built near the ocean where ships could bring them needed supplies. After early missions began to grow their own food and care for themselves, later mission compounds were built farther away from the coast. What one mission did well, such as leatherworking, candlemaking, or raising cattle, was shared with other missions. As a result, missions became somewhat specialized in certain products.

Although mission buildings looked different from mission to mission, most were built from one basic plan. Usually a compound was constructed as a large, four-sided building with an inner patio in the center. The outside of the quadrangle had only one or two doors, which were locked at night to protect the mission. A church usually sat at one corner of the quadrangle and was always the tallest and largest part of the mission compound.

Facing the inner patio were rooms for the two priests living there, workshops, a kitchen, storage rooms for grain and food, and the mission office. Rooms along the back of the quadrangle often served as home to the unmarried Indian women who worked in the kitchen. The rest of the Indians lived just outside the walls of the mission in their own village.

Beyond the mission wall and next to the church was a cemetery. Today you can still see many of the original headstones of those who died while living and working at the mission. Also outside the walls were larger workshops, a reservoir holding water used at the mission, and orchards containing fruit trees. Huge fields surrounded each mission where crops grew and livestock such as sheep, cattle, and horses grazed.

It took a great deal of time for some Indian tribes to understand the new way of life a mission offered, even though the Native Americans always had food and shelter when they became mission Indians. Each morning all Indians were awakened at sunrise by a church bell calling them to church. Breakfast followed church . . . and then work. The women spun thread and made clothes, as well as cooked meals. Men and older boys worked in workshops or fields and constructed buildings. Meanwhile the Indian children went to school, where the padres taught them. After a noon meal there was a two hour rest before work began again. After dinner the Indians sang, played, or danced. This way of life was an enormous change from the less organized Indian life before the missionaries arrived. Many tribes accepted the change, some had more trouble getting used to a regular schedule, some tribes never became a part of mission life.

Water was all-important to the missions. It was needed to irrigate crops and to provide for the mission people and animals. Priests designed and engineered magnificent irrigation systems at most of the missions. All building of aqueducts and reservoirs of these systems was done by the mission Indians.

With all the organized hard work, the missions did very well. They grew and became strong. Excellent vineyards gave wine for the priests to use and to sell. Mission fields produced large grain crops of wheat and corn, and vast grazing land developed huge herds of cattle and sheep. Mission life was successful for over fifty years.

When Mexico broke away from Spain, it found it did not have enough money to support the California missions, as Spain had been doing. So in 1834, Mexico enforced the secularization law which their government had decreed several years earlier. This law stated missions were to be taken away from the missionaries and given to the Indians. The law said that if an Indian did not want the land or buildings, the property was to be sold to anyone who wished to buy it.

It is true the missions had become quite large and powerful. And as shocked as the padres were to learn of the secularization law, they also knew the missions had originally been planned as temporary, or short term projects. The priests had been sure their Indians would be well-trained enough to run the missions by themselves when the time came to move to other unsettled lands. In fact, however, even after fifty years the California Indians were still not ready to handle the huge missions.

Since the Indians did not wish to continue the missions, the buildings and land were sold, the Indians not even waiting for money or, in some cases, receiving money for the sale.

Sad times lay ahead. Many Indians went back to the old way of life. Some Indians stayed on as servants to the new owners and often these owners were not good to them. Mission buildings were used for everything from stores and saloons to animal barns. In one mission the church became a barracks for the army. A balcony was built for soldiers with their horses stabled in the altar area. Rats ate the stored grain and beautiful church robes. Furniture and objects left by the padres were stolen. People even stole the mission building roof tiles, which then caused the adobe brick walls to melt from rain. Earthquakes finished off many buildings.

Shortly after California became a part of the United States in the mid-1850s, our government returned all mission buildings to the Catholic Church. By this time most of them were in terrible condition. Since the priests needed only the church itself and a few rooms to live in, the other rooms of the mission were rented to anyone who needed them. Strange uses were found in some cases. In the San Fernando Mission, for example, there was once a pig farm in the patio area.

Tourists finally began to notice the mission ruins in the early 1900s. Groups of interested people got together to see if the missions could be restored. Some missions had been "modernized" by this time, unfortunately, but within the last thirty years historians have found enough pictures, drawings, and written descriptions to rebuild or restore most of the missions to their original appearances.

The restoration of all twenty-one missions is a splendid way to preserve our California heritage. It is the hope of many Californians that this dream of restoration can become a reality in the near future.

*Beautiful reredos built by Harry Downie to look like the 1849 reredos. Fr. Serra is buried inside the altar rail, to the left of the main altar.*

# MISSION SAN CARLOS BORROMEO de CARMELO

## I. THE MISSION TODAY

Mission San Carlos Borromeo de Carmelo is often simply called the Carmel Mission. It sits at the edge of the town of Carmel, surrounded by fine homes, near where the Carmel River empties into Carmel Bay and the Pacific Ocean. The mission compound has been beautifully restored by Mr. Harry Downie, an excellent craftsman who spent most of his life rebuilding Mission San Carlos. As a result of his dedication, the Carmel Mission church is one of the most authentically restored of all the mission churches in California. In 1960 it was raised to the level of a minor basilica church because of the important part it played in the life of Fr. Junipero Serra, founder of the California Mission Chain.

The front, or facade, of the church is rather Moorish in style and is easily recognized in pictures by the unique star window above the entrance doors. The walls of the present church are of native brown sandstone. Mortar between the stones was made from the lime in abalone shells found on the beach nearby. Five feet thick at the base, the walls at one time widened to form an innerwall curve which forms the arch of the thirty-three foot high ceiling. Today the restored ceiling is formed by redwood planks painted to look like the original stone.

Two unalike towers sit at the top of the facade. The larger tower holds eight mission bells, most of which are original. The courtyard in front of the church is bright with colorful flower gardens.

The inside of the church is lovely. A baptistry is to the left of the entrance at the back of the church. Inside the baptistry is the original stone baptismal font. Also, to the left, but much larger, is the old mortuary chapel, now called Belem Chapel. Above the altar in this chapel is the restored Our Lady of Belem (Bethlehem) statue, a favorite of Father Serra's. Two families cared for the statue during long years when the mission lay in ruins. It was returned to the church in 1948 and placed in the chapel named for it.

On the walls of the main part of the church are framed, painted Stations of the Cross. There are six gold-plated, crystal chandeliers hanging from the vaulted ceiling. High on the right wall is the restored pulpit. Mr. Downie carved the pulpit to look as much like the original as possible. Fresco painting, done in gold, is found on the upper part of the side walls. High windows along the walls are glass-paned in many colors.

There is a magnificent reredos on the back wall of the sanctuary, which was carved and shaped to fit the wall. Mr. Downie hand-carved the great reredos himself in 1956, using the style of the Mission Dolores reredos in San Francisco. He did his best to carve it like the original one that stood on the same spot until 1849. Several original polychromed (paint on wood) statues are placed in the reredos. At the top stands a dove representing the Holy Spirit.

A small umbrella showing the church to be a Minor Basilica sits on the floor to the right of the main altar.

Beside the church, to the right, is the old walled cemetery. Among graves of mounded dirt bordered with sea shells is a monument of a cross and two spears that represents the 2,346 Indians and 14 Spaniards buried there between 1771 and 1833.

To the left side of the church is the fully rebuilt quadrangle and patio. Instead of faithfully restoring the workshop side of the quadrangle, however, a modern elementary school has been built within the restored adobe walls. The front of the quadrangle houses those priests living at the mission. A part of the front wall of the priests' quarters is the only original wall left standing from mission days. This portion has not been replastered so all may see it.

The northeast corner of the quadrangle has been carefully

restored and contains a gift shop and a museum of rooms once used by Fr. Serra and his assistant, Father Juan Crespí. The museum rooms are so well restored that one feels as though Fr. Serra were just away for a moment. There is a recreated kitchen, dining room, common room, and library with some of Fr. Serra's original books. Most interesting is the recreation of Fr. Serra's bedroom-cell. Harry Downie used a written description of the padre's room as it was in 1784 to furnish the cell. Father Serra's good friend, Fr. Francisco Palóu, had included a complete description of the almost bare cell in a biography he wrote of Fr. Serra's life in the late 1700s. No wonder the cell looks so authentic.

At one end of the museum is a special chapel room containing some of the original robes used by Fray Serra. Also on display are silver candelabras, Fr. Serra's silver chalice, and other items used for church events. In the center of the narrow room is a magnificent sarcophagus sculptured by artisan Jo Mora in 1924 in honor of Fr. Serra. A sarcophagus is a stone coffin often left empty and placed over the ground where a body is buried. It was first planned that the sarcophagus would be placed over the grave of Fr. Serra in the sanctuary of the church. However, the coffin with the life-size bronze figure of Fr. Serra on the top, and three life-size bronze statues of Franciscan monks praying about it, is on a twelve foot by eight foot base. It was far too large to be put in the church, so a special room in the museum was given over to this fine sculpture.

The Basilica of Carmel Mission is visited by over two hundred thousand people each year, a tribute to what many feel is the most beautiful California mission church of all.

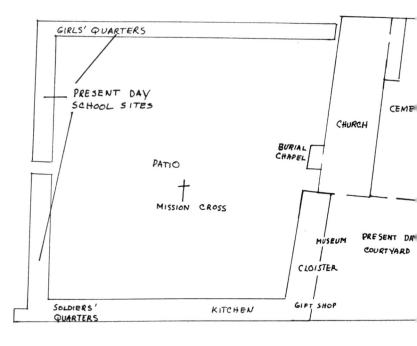

GIRLS' QUARTERS

PRESENT DAY
SCHOOL SITES

CHURCH

CEME

PATIO

BURIAL
CHAPEL

✝

MISSION CROSS

MUSEUM

PRESENT DA
COURTYARD

CLOISTER

SOLDIERS'
QUARTERS

KITCHEN

GIFT SHOP

SAN CARLOS DE BORROMEOS DE CARMELO

RESTORED QUADRANGLE

14

## II.  HISTORY OF THE MISSION

Mission San Carlos Borromeo de Carmelo was founded June 3, 1770, by Fr. Junípero Serra at the Presidio of Monterey. The mission was named in honor of Saint Charles Borromeo, Archbishop of Milan, who died in 1538. It took Fr. Serra less than a year to realize that his mission site did not have enough water, had poor soil, and worst of all, was far too close to the rowdy soldiers of the presidio.

Fray Serra searched the hills around him and decided the best site for the mission would be near the Carmel River, about six miles to the south. In the summer of 1771, building was begun by forty Indians from Baja (lower) California missions, three soldiers, and five sailors. Fr. Serra took complete charge, for this was to be his headquarters in the development of the mission chain, and he wanted it to be just right.

The first buildings, except for the church, were made of logs stuck into the ground to form walls. Other logs were laid across the top. A mat of sticks and a covering of grass covered the ceiling of logs. The church was only a brush hut put alongside the large wooden cross Fr. Serra erected on the site. Around these buildings was a palisade or pole fence.

Although some farm animals had been brought to the new mission, there were not enough to provide food for all the people in the mission. Crops had not yet been planted, so the first winter was a terrible, starving time. No ships were able to sail north with supplies because of the strong winter winds and storms. The mission people might have died if a group of soldiers had not traveled south and successfully hunted bears. The bear meat, plus some seeds harvested at Mission San Antonio, kept the Carmel Mission alive until a ship arrived at Monterey.

Father Serra went with the bear hunters, founding Mission San Luis Obispo in the Valley of the Bears; then went on to San Diego just in time to convince a Spanish sea captain he must sail northward with supplies to help the Fr.'s starving mission.

In the year and a half that Fr. Serra was in San Diego and Mexico, Father Palóu started the building of a new church of logs and tule. Fr. Palóu was an excellent gardener as well, and he began a vegetable garden that was to be the beginning of California's huge lettuce and artichoke farms of today.

In early 1774, supplies once again ran low and the mission people almost died. But by harvest time that year there were 207 bushels of wheat, 250 bushels of corn, and 45 bushels of beans raised to help supply the mission's needs. In 1775 the harvest was four times greater, nearly enough to actually care for the mission at Carmel. A man named Don Juan Bautista de Anza finally began bringing supplies by land to the missions about this time, so they no longer had to depend on ships alone for their needs.

By 1776, the mission had grown. It had a well-made church of palisades and tule. The padres' quarters were now built of adobe with three good-sized rooms, and there was even a separate kitchen.

An adobe church was built in 1782 to take the place of Fr. Palóu's log and tule church. Fr. Crespi, Father Serra's life-long friend, was soon to be buried in the new adobe church. In 1783 there were 700 persons living at the mission and its rancheria. An irrigation canal had been constructed from the Carmel River to a pool near the mission for keeping fish alive. The Indians were now trained plowmen, shepherds, cattle herders, blacksmiths and carpenters. Within the mission Indian workers were making adobe bricks, roof tiles, and the tools they needed.

On August 28, 1784, Father Junípero Serra laid down his tired body in his bare room at the mission and died. He was buried beside Fr. Crespi in the sanctuary of the adobe church. Before he died, however, he had made sure that a stone church would be built.

Father Fermin Lasuén, who took Fr. Serra's place as Father-presidente of the California missions, decided to go ahead with the stone church in 1793. The new church was to be built exactly where the adobe church was, so the graves of Frs. Serra and Crespi would not have to be moved. A master mason (brick-layer), Manuel Ruiz, was brought from Mexico to take charge of the construction.

The great church was finished and dedicated in 1797. By 1803

Fr. Lasuén was himself buried next to Fr. Serra and Fr. Crespi in the sanctuary of the new stone church.

In 1834, secularization laws took the mission away from the hardworking priests. The new Mexican government sold the Carmel Mission land — right up to the walls of the church! The church roof collapsed in 1851, and the building was roofless for the next thirty years. Even after the roof had fallen, though, church services were often held among the debris of the ruined building.

In the year 1884, Fr. Angelo Casanova, the pastor of the nearby Monterey church, raised money to repair the mission church. He wanted the church to be reroofed for the one hundredth anniversary of the death of Father Serra. Enough money was raised for the roof, but unfortunately the shingle roof that was built to cover the church was very tall, coming to a high peak at the top. The entire look of the beautiful stone church was changed by this strange-looking roof. Even so, it remained in place until 1936, when Mr. Downie, restorer of the mission, rebuilt the roof like the original. Once again San Carlos church had a gracefully arched roof covered in red tiles.

Some words must be said about Mr. Harry Downie. His real name was Henry John Downie and he started working at Mission San Carlos only as a repairman of broken statues. But he became so interested in the history of the mission that he began to research all he could find on the destroyed buildings of the original mission quadrangle. By 1931, he had begun to faithfully rebuild some parts of the mission proper. Mr. Downie began by restoring the northeast corner of the quadrangle. This is the museum we see today. Next he lowered and drained the front courtyard so the church would not flood each time it rained. His third project was to replace the ugly shingle roof of the church which had been there since 1884.

Slowly the quadrangle was fully restored. In 1939, Mr. Downie discovered the remains of the original wooden cross Fr. Serra had placed there in 1771. The site was in the patio area near the museum wing. He studied drawings from mission days and carefully formed a cross like the first one. When you visit the mission you can see a tall wooden cross sitting in the exact same spot Fr. Serra placed the old one so long ago.

For over fifty years the dedicated draftsman, Harry Downie, lovingly rebuilt the beautiful Mission San Carlos Borromeo de Carmelo so that when we visit the mission today, we see Father Serra's favorite place as he would have loved it — a working and productive place.

*Original library at San Carlos has been restored. It was the first library in California. The original books here were Fray Serra's own, brought by him in late 1770's.*

# OUTLINE OF
## SAN CARLOS BORROMEO de CARMELO

**I. The mission today**
- A. Location
- B. Restored by Harry Downie
- C. Church is  minor basilica
  - 1. Historic importance
- D. Church exterior
  - 1. Style of facade
  - 2. Star window
  - 3. Standstone walls
  - 4. Mortar
  - 5. Towers not alike
    - a. Bells
  - 6. Courtyard
- E. Church interior
  - 1. Baptistry and baptismal font
  - 2. Belem Chapel
    - a. Stations of the Cross
    - b. Chandeliers
    - c. Restored pulpit
    - d. High windows
  - 4. Reredos
    - a. Carved by whom?
    - b. Style of Dolores
    - c. Like pictures of original
    - d. Statues
    - e. Dove
  - 5. Umbrella of Basilica
- F. Cemetery
  - 1. Monument to Indians buried there
- G. Quadrangle
  - 1. Outside walls fully restored
  - 2. Elementary school on workshop side
  - 3. Priests' quarters
    - a. Original wall
  - 4. Museum corner or quadrangle
    - a. Different rooms contained in it (Serra's cell)
    - b. Sarcophagus room

*Outline continued next page*

## II. History of mission

A. Founding
1. Date
2. Founder
B. Moving of mission to Carmel River
C. First buildings
1. Church
D. First winter
1. No supplies
2. Bear hunt and seeds
3. Fr. Serra founds San Luis Obispo - San Diego
E. Fr. Palóu's garden and church
F. 1774
1. First harvest
G. 1775
1. Larger harvest
2. de Anza's supplies
H. Mission in 1776
I. Adobe church
1. Fr. Crespí's burial
J. 1783 at the mission
K. Fr. Serra's death and burial
L. Father Lasuén
1. Stone church built
2. Graves of Serra and Crespí
3. Lasuén's death and burial
M. Secularization in 1834
1. Ruin of the mission
N. 1884
1. Fr. Casanova's new roof
O. Harry Downie's restoration
1. Museum
2. Replacement of shingle roof
3. Whole quadrangle restored
4. Wooden cross of Fr. Serra
P. Ending

# GLOSSARY

**BUTTRESS:** a large mass of stone or wood used to strengthen buildings

**CAMPANARIO:** a wall which holds bells

**CLOISTER:** an enclosed area; a word often used instead of convento

**CONVENTO:** mission building where priests lived

**CORRIDOR:** covered, outside hallway found at most missions

**EL CAMINO REAL:** highway between missions; also known as The King's Highway

**FACADE:** front wall of a building

**FONT:** large, often decorated bowl containing Holy Water for baptizing people

**FOUNDATION:** base of a building, part of which is below the ground

**FRESCO:** designs painted directly on walls or ceilings

**LEGEND:** a story coming from the past

**PORTICO:** porch or covered outside hallway

**PRESERVE:** to keep in good condition without change

**PRESIDIO:** a settlement of military men

**QUADRANGLE:** four-sided shape; the shape of most missions

**RANCHOS:** large ranches often many miles from mission proper where crops were grown and animal herds grazed

**REBUILD:** to build again; to repair a great deal of something

**REPLICA:** a close copy of the original

**REREDOS:** the wall behind the main altar inside the church

**\*RESTORATION:** to bring something back to its original condition (see * below)

**SANCTUARY:** area inside, at the front of the church where the main altar is found

**SECULARIZATION:** something not religious; a law in mission days taking the mission buildings away from the church and placing them under government rule

**\*ORIGINAL:** the first one; the first one built

# BIBLIOGRAPHY

Bauer, Helen. *California Mission Days.* Sacramento, CA: California State Department of Education, 1957.

Goodman, Marian. *Missions of California.* Redwood City, CA: Redwood City Tribune, 1962.

Pamphlet. *Mission San Carlos Borromeo.* Boston, MA 02130-4598: Colourpicture Publishing, Inc., no date.

Sunset Editors. *The California Missions.* Menlo Park, CA: Lane Publishing Company, 1979.

Temple, Sydney. *The Carmel Mission from Founding to Rebuilding.* Fresno, CA 93728: Valley Publishers (Div. of Book Publishers, Ind.), 1980.

Weber, Msgr. Francis J. *Father of the Mission.* Hong Kong: Libra Press Limited, no date.

Wright, Ralph B., ed. *California Missions.* Arroyo Grande, CA 93420: Hubert A. Lowman, 1978.

For more information about this mission, write to:

> Mission San Carlos Borremeo
> Carmel, CA 93923

It is best to enclose a self-addressed, stamped envelope and a small amount of money to pay for brochures and pictures the mission might send you.

## CREDITS

Cover art and Father Serra Illustration: Ellen Grim
Illustrations: Alfredo de Batuc
Gound Layout: Mary Boulé

SAN FRANCISCO SOLANO
(Sonoma)

SAN RAFAEL ARCÁNGEL

SAN FRANCISCO DE ASÍS

SAN JOSÉ
(Fremont)

SANTA CLARA

SANTA CRUZ

SAN JUAN BAUTISTA

SAN CARLOS DE BORROMEO DE CARMELO
(Carmel)

NUESTRA SENORA DE LA SOLEDAD

SAN ANTONIO DE PADUA
(Jolon)

SAN MIGUEL ARCÁNGEL

SAN LUIS OBISPO DE TOLOSA

LA PURISIMA CONCEPCIÓN
(Lompoc)

SANTA INÉS

SANTA BÁRBARA

SAN BUENAVENTURA
(Ventura)

SAN FERNANDO REY DE ESPANA

SAN GABRIEL ARCÁNGEL

PACIFIC
OCEAN

SAN JUAN CAPISTRANO

SAN LUIS REY DE FRANCIA

SAN DIEGO DE ALCALÁ

NAME OF CITY IN PARENTHESES, IF OTHER THAN MISSION NAME

*At last, a  detailed book on the*

*Mission San  Carlos  Borromeo*

*de Carmelo  written  just for students*

## ABOUT THE AUTHOR

Mary Null Boulé has taught in the California Public School System for 25 years. Her past ten years as a fourth grade teacher made her aware of the necessity for a detailed informational book about the California missions. Five years of research, including visits to each mission, have resulted in this excellent series.

She is married and the mother of five grown children.

ISBN: 1-877599-01-8